101 FACTS ABOUT OLIVIA RODRIGO

The Unofficial Kid and Teen Quiz & Trivia Guide to the Amazing Popstar

Tessa Temecula

Did you know?

1: Olivia Rodrigo Was Born to Shine

Imagine being able to sing, act, and write songs all before you're even a teenager. Pretty amazing, right? Well, that's exactly what Olivia Rodrigo did! Born on February 20, 2003, in Murrieta, California, Olivia started her journey to superstardom early on. Her parents, Jennifer and Chris, noticed Olivia's love for music and acting, so they immediately signed her up for lessons. She began taking singing lessons, learning piano and eventually adding acting to her list of talents. Little did she know, those early lessons would kick-start a career that would make her one of the most famous young stars in the world. Can you imagine where you'll be when you're Olivia's age?

2: Proud of Her Filipino Heritage

Something special about Olivia that not everyone might know is that she's incredibly proud of her Filipino heritage! Her great-grandfather moved to the United States from the Philippines, and Olivia has always embraced that part of her background. In fact, she and her family still celebrate Filipino traditions and enjoy delicious Filipino cuisine. Olivia's connection to her heritage is important to her, and it's a big reason why she's so relatable to fans worldwide. Isn't it cool to see a star who embraces all the parts of who they are?

3: Olivia's Disney Channel Days

You might know Olivia as a superstar musician. Still, before she topped the charts, she made people laugh on the Disney Channel! Olivia played Paige Olvera, a fun-loving, guitar-playing character on Bizaardvark, a show that ran from 2016 to 2019. Paige and her best friend were all about creating music videos and posting them online. Sound familiar? Kind of like real life for Olivia, right? This role allowed her to show off her acting skills to a young audience and paved the way for her next big break. If you ever watched Bizaardvark, you probably got a glimpse of Olivia's star power before she became the pop sensation we know today!

4: Nini Salazar-Roberts Changin Everything

After Bizaardvark, Olivia landed a role that would change her life forever–Nini Salazar-Roberts in High School Musical: The Musical: The Series. The Disney+ show was a huge hit, and Olivia's character was a major part of its success. What made this role even more special? Olivia acted in the show and wrote and performed one of its most popular songs, "All I Want." Fans loved the song so much that it became a chart-topping hit on its own! Nini was a relatable character who loved performing, just like Olivia in real life. Through this role, Olivia proved she wasn't just an actress–she was a multi-talented force ready to take on the world.

Did you know?

5: The Breakthrough Single-"Drivers License"

Let's talk about the moment that made Olivia a household name-the release of "Drivers License." You've probably heard the song a million times (it's one of those tracks you can't help but play on repeat), but did you know it made history? When Olivia released "Drivers License" in January 2021, it broke Spotify streaming records twice in one week! It hit over 17 million streams daily and over 80 million in just seven days. Talk about taking the music world by storm! The song went straight to number one on the Billboard Hot 100, making Olivia the youngest artist to debut at the top of the chart. Whether you're listening to it for the first time or the 50th, "Drivers License" still hits just as hard, doesn't it?

6: Olivia Owns Her Music

Here's something that makes Olivia slightly different from other young artists-she has serious business smarts. When Olivia signed with Geffen Records in 2020, she made sure she owned the masters of her music. What does that mean? It means Olivia controls her songs, a rare move for young artists. Most singers don't get to own their masters until later in their careers (if ever), but Olivia made sure she had control right from the start. She knew how important it was to keep ownership of the music she worked so hard to create. That's pretty awesome, right? It shows that Olivia isn't just talented-she's smart, too!

Did you know?

7: The Inspiration Behind "Sour"

Olivia's debut album, Sour, is packed with emotion, heartbreak, and relatable lyrics that seem to speak to everyone who listens. But where did all that inspiration come from? According to Olivia, writing Sour was like therapy for her. She poured all her feelings into the songs, turning real-life experiences into music that connected with fans in a big way. Whether it's the raw emotion of "Drivers License" or the fiery energy of "Good 4 U," Sour became the soundtrack for a generation of listeners who felt like Olivia was singing directly to them. And guess what? That was exactly her goal. Have you ever listened to a song and felt like it was written just for you?

8: A Record-Breaking Tour

After the release of Sour, fans couldn't wait to see Olivia live in concert. When the Sour Tour was announced, it sold out in record time! Olivia performed in cities across the United States, Canada, and Europe, bringing her songs to life on stage. Concertgoers raved about the energy and emotion she brought to every performance, and it was clear that Olivia's music wasn't just meant to be listened to-it was meant to be experienced. For many fans, attending one of her concerts was a dream come true, and Olivia made sure to give her all at every single show. Have you ever been to a concert that left you speechless?

9: A Huge Taylor Swift Fan

Olivia is a self-proclaimed Swiftie, and she doesn't hide it! From an early age, Taylor Swift was one of Olivia's biggest inspirations for songwriting. In interviews, Olivia has shared how much she admires Taylor's ability to tell stories through her songs, something she strives to do in her own music. In fact, when Sour was released, fans noticed a special nod to Taylor in Olivia's song "1 Step Forward, 3 Steps Back," which even sampled from Taylor's song "New Year's Day." What's even cooler? Taylor gave Olivia a shout-out on social media after hearing "Drivers License." Imagine getting recognition from your musical hero! Talk about a dream come true.

10: Making History at the Grammys

The Grammy Awards are like the Oscars of music, and Olivia didn't just attend-she won big! At the 2022 Grammy Awards, Olivia took home three of the biggest trophies: Best New Artist, Best Pop Solo Performance for "Drivers License," and Best Pop Vocal Album for Sour. This made her one of the youngest artists to win such major categories at a single Grammy ceremony. Seeing Olivia on stage, smiling with her awards in hand, was a moment that her fans (and probably Olivia herself) will never forget. It's proof that her music has touched the hearts of millions-and that she's just getting started.

11: Breaking Records with "Good 4 U"

You've probably jammed out to Olivia's upbeat anthem "Good 4 U" at least once-who hasn't? But did you know that this song was a record-breaker? Released in May 2021, "Good 4 U" debuted at number one on the Billboard Hot 100, making it Olivia's second number-one hit after "Drivers License." What's even cooler is that "Good 4 U" showed Olivia's versatility as an artist. While "Drivers License" was a heart-wrenching ballad, "Good 4 U" had that punchy, rebellious energy that made it impossible not to sing along. Whether you're feeling all the feels or just need a song to dance to, Olivia's got you covered!

12: From Acting to Singing-A Big Career Move

Even though Olivia made a name for herself on Disney Channel, she always knew that music was her true passion. After starring in High School Musical: The Musical: The Series, Olivia left the show to focus on her music career full-time. It was a huge risk, but it totally paid off! Since shifting her focus to music, Olivia has become one of the biggest pop stars in the world. Her story is a great reminder that sometimes, even when scary, following your passion can lead to amazing things. Have you ever made a big decision that changed everything for you?

Show Off Your Olivia Smarts!

1. What was Olivia's debut single that skyrocketed her to fame in 2021?

A) Good 4 U
B) Deja Vu
C) Drivers License
D) Traitor

2. Which Disney+ series did Olivia star in from 2019 to 2022?

A) Bizaardvark
B) High School Musical: The Musical: The Series
C) Hannah Montana
D) Andi Mack

Did you know?

13: A Talented Songwriter

Olivia is more than just an amazing singer and a gifted songwriter. In fact, she writes or co-writes all of her songs, which is rare for young pop stars. Olivia's lyrics are known for being super relatable and emotional, which is why so many of her fans connect with her music on a deep level. Whether she's writing about heartbreak, self-discovery, or the ups and downs of growing up, Olivia pours her heart into every song. Next time you listen to one of her tracks, pay close attention to the lyrics- you might find a line that speaks directly to your feelings!

14: Olivia's Musical Inspirations

When you listen to Olivia's music, you can hear influences from some of her favorite artists. Along with Taylor Swift, Olivia has mentioned that she looks up to musicians like Lorde, Alanis Morissette, and Fiona Apple. She also grew up listening to alternative rock bands like No Doubt, Green Day, and Pearl Jam, which is why some of her songs have a cool, edgy vibe. Olivia loves artists who are honest and bold in their music, and she brings that same energy to her own songs. Who knows-maybe one day we'll talk about how Olivia inspired the next generation of musicians!

Did you know?

15: Olivia's Documentary, Driving Home 2 U

Ever wondered what it's like to create an album? Olivia gave her fans a behind-the-scenes look at her journey with the release of her 2022 documentary Olivia Rodrigo: Driving Home 2 U. The film shows the making of her debut album, Sour, and takes fans on a road trip through the creative process, from writing the songs to recording them. It's an emotional and inspiring look at how Olivia turned her thoughts and feelings into music with which the whole world fell in love. If you haven't watched it yet, it's a must-see for any Olivia fan who wants to understand her journey better!

16: Time's Entertainer of the Year

In 2021, Olivia was named Time Magazine's Entertainer of the Year, an honor given to only the biggest and most impactful stars. This was a huge deal, especially since Olivia launched her music career that year. Time recognized Olivia not only for her incredible music but also for how she resonated with fans worldwide. At just 18 years old, Olivia had become a voice for a generation, using her songs to express feelings that so many people could relate to. Can you imagine being named Entertainer of the Year at such a young age? Olivia sure made history!

Did you know?

17: Olivia's Charity Work

Even though Olivia is super busy with her music and acting, she still makes time to give back. In 2023, she launched her charity, Fund 4 Good, which supports important causes like reproductive healthcare for women. Olivia has also donated proceeds from her tours and merchandise to organizations that help people in need. She's shown that she's an amazing artist and someone who cares deeply about making a difference in the world. It's inspiring to see a young star use their platform for good.

18: The Guts Era-Olivia's Second Album

In 2023, Olivia returned with her highly anticipated second album, Guts. Suppose Sour was all about heartbreak and growing up. In that case, Guts is about self-discovery and the challenges of becoming an adult. Olivia has said that she felt like she "grew ten years" between the ages of 18 and 20 and that growth is reflected in the album's lyrics. With songs like "Vampire" and "Bad Idea Right?", Guts shows off a more mature and confident side of Olivia. Fans and critics loved the album, and it quickly topped the charts, proving that Olivia's star power is here to stay.

19: Olivia's First Song-At Just Five Years Old!

Here's a fun fact that'll surprise you-Olivia wrote her first song when she was five years old! She titled "The Bels," a cute little Christmas tune she shared with her fans in 2021. She even posted a snippet of it on Instagram, and let's just say it's adorable! Imagine writing your own song at five-some serious talent, even at a young age. It's no wonder Olivia grew up to be a pop sensation. Who knows, maybe that early songwriting practice helped her become the amazing lyricist she is today. Do you remember what you were doing when you were five?

20: A Love for Poetry

Not only is Olivia an incredible songwriter, but she's also got a love for poetry. In fact, while working on her second album, Guts, she took a poetry class at the University of Southern California. One of the poems she wrote in that class inspired her song "Lacy," which was featured on the album. It's cool to see how her poetry skills crossed over into her music, giving her lyrics extra depth and emotion. You'll notice some poetic flair next time you listen to her songs!

21: Olivia's "Sour Prom" Concert Film

Who says prom has to be all about fancy dresses and slow dances? Olivia gave fans a prom experience when she released Sour Prom, a concert film inspired by the music from her debut album. The film, which premiered on YouTube in June 2021, was full of emotional performances and prom-themed fun. Dressed in her prom best, Olivia performed songs from Sour, bringing the album to life in a totally unique way. Whether or not you've been to prom, Sour Prom was the perfect way to experience Olivia's music in a new light. Have you checked it out yet?

22: The Youngest BRIT Billion Award Winner

Olivia's accomplishments just keep piling up! In 2023, she became the youngest artist ever to receive the BRIT Billion Award, given to artists reaching over one billion streams in the UK. It's a massive achievement showing how popular Olivia's music has become worldwide. She's already breaking records left and right with only two albums under her belt. Pretty amazing, right? It's exciting to think about what other milestones she'll reach as her career soars.

Did you know?

23: Olivia's Style Evolution

When Olivia first stepped onto the scene, she wowed fans with her music and unique sense of style. From her edgy Sour era looks, filled with '90s-inspired plaid skirts and chunky boots, to the more polished and grown-up fashion choices during her Guts era, Olivia has shown that her style evolves just like her music. She's been known to mix high fashion with thrift store finds, making her look cool and relatable. It's no wonder she's become a fashion icon for many of her fans. Which of Olivia's style eras do you love the most?

24: A Connection to The Hunger Games

Here's a fact that fans of The Hunger Games franchise will love! In 2023, Olivia wrote and performed a song called "Can't Catch Me Now" for the movie The Hunger Games: The Ballad of Songbirds & Snakes. The song was a huge hit with both fans and critics, and it even won a Hollywood Music in Media Award for Best Original Song in a Sci-Fi, Fantasy, or Horror Film. Olivia's ability to create a song that fits perfectly with The Hunger Games's dark, intense world is just one more example of her talent. If you're a fan of the movies, this is definitely a song worth listening to!

Show Off Your Olivia Smarts!

3. What year was Olivia named Time magazine's Entertainer of the Year?

A) 2020
B) 2021
C) 2022
D) 2023

4. Which song from Olivia's Sour album was inspired by watching TV shows?

A) Good 4 U
B) Brutal
C) Deja Vu
D) Favorite Crime

Did you know?

25: Olivia's Grammy-Winning Single "Drivers License"

We already know that "Drivers License" was a record-breaking hit, but did you know it also won a Grammy? At the 2022 Grammy Awards, Olivia took home the Best Pop Solo Performance trophy thanks to this emotional ballad. The song became an anthem for anyone going through heartbreak, and its raw lyrics and haunting melody struck a chord with listeners everywhere. Olivia's song performance at the Grammy ceremony was one of the night's highlights, showcasing her ability to connect with audiences through her voice and her words. Have you ever listened to "Drivers License" on repeat after a tough day?

26: Supporting Women Through "Fund 4 Good"

Olivia's talent isn't the only thing that makes her stand out-her big heart does, too. In 2023, she launched a nonprofit organization called Fund 4 Good, which supports causes like women's reproductive healthcare and other important issues affecting women. Part of the proceeds from her Guts tour goes directly to this fund, showing that Olivia is dedicated to using her platform for positive change. Seeing someone as young as Olivia making such a big difference in the world is inspiring. Wouldn't it be amazing if more celebrities followed in her footsteps?

Did you know?

21: Olivia's "Sour Prom" Concert Film

Who says prom has to be all about fancy dresses and slow dances? Olivia gave fans a prom experience when she released Sour Prom, a concert film inspired by the music from her debut album. The film, which premiered on YouTube in June 2021, was full of emotional performances and prom-themed fun. Dressed in her prom best, Olivia performed songs from Sour, bringing the album to life in a totally unique way. Whether or not you've been to prom, Sour Prom was the perfect way to experience Olivia's music in a new light. Have you checked it out yet?

22: The Youngest BRIT Billion Award Winner

Olivia's accomplishments just keep piling up! In 2023, she became the youngest artist ever to receive the BRIT Billion Award, given to artists reaching over one billion streams in the UK. It's a massive achievement showing how popular Olivia's music has become worldwide. She's already breaking records left and right with only two albums under her belt. Pretty amazing, right? It's exciting to think about what other milestones she'll reach as her career soars.

Did you know?

23: Olivia's Style Evolution

When Olivia first stepped onto the scene, she wowed fans with her music and unique sense of style. From her edgy Sour era looks, filled with '90s-inspired plaid skirts and chunky boots, to the more polished and grown-up fashion choices during her Guts era, Olivia has shown that her style evolves just like her music. She's been known to mix high fashion with thrift store finds, making her look cool and relatable. It's no wonder she's become a fashion icon for many of her fans. Which of Olivia's style eras do you love the most?

24: A Connection to The Hunger Games

Here's a fact that fans of The Hunger Games franchise will love! In 2023, Olivia wrote and performed a song called "Can't Catch Me Now" for the movie The Hunger Games: The Ballad of Songbirds & Snakes. The song was a huge hit with both fans and critics, and it even won a Hollywood Music in Media Award for Best Original Song in a Sci-Fi, Fantasy, or Horror Film. Olivia's ability to create a song that fits perfectly with The Hunger Games's dark, intense world is just one more example of her talent. If you're a fan of the movies, this is definitely a song worth listening to!

Did you know?

25: Olivia's Grammy-Winning Single "Drivers License"

We already know that "Drivers License" was a record-breaking hit, but did you know it also won a Grammy? At the 2022 Grammy Awards, Olivia took home the Best Pop Solo Performance trophy thanks to this emotional ballad. The song became an anthem for anyone going through heartbreak, and its raw lyrics and haunting melody struck a chord with listeners everywhere. Olivia's song performance at the Grammy ceremony was one of the night's highlights, showcasing her ability to connect with audiences through her voice and her words. Have you ever listened to "Drivers License" on repeat after a tough day?

26: Supporting Women Through "Fund 4 Good"

Olivia's talent isn't the only thing that makes her stand out-her big heart does, too. In 2023, she launched a nonprofit organization called Fund 4 Good, which supports causes like women's reproductive healthcare and other important issues affecting women. Part of the proceeds from her Guts tour goes directly to this fund, showing that Olivia is dedicated to using her platform for positive change. Seeing someone as young as Olivia making such a big difference in the world is inspiring. Wouldn't it be amazing if more celebrities followed in her footsteps?

Did you know?

27: Olivia's Big Move to Los Angeles

At just 12 years old, Olivia made a huge decision: she moved to Los Angeles from her hometown in Murrieta, California, to pursue her acting career full-time. It was a bold move, but one that clearly paid off! Leaving her friends and familiar surroundings behind was challenging. Still, Olivia's determination to chase her dreams is one of the things that makes her such an inspiring role model. Living in LA opened up countless opportunities for her, including landing her roles on Disney Channel and Disney+. Can you imagine moving to a big city at 12? It's a pretty big deal!

28: Olivia Loves Vintage Shopping

When Olivia isn't on stage or in the studio, you might find her browsing through thrift stores! She has said that she loves vintage shopping and often searches for cool, one-of-a-kind pieces. Some of her best fashion finds have come from secondhand stores, where she mixes high-end style with affordable, unique items. Olivia's thrifty fashion sense has made her a style icon for fans who love finding their own looks at vintage stores. It's a great reminder that you don't need to spend a fortune to look fabulous! Do you have a favorite thrift store find?

29: Olivia's Role in Promoting COVID-19 Vaccines

In 2021, Olivia teamed up with the White House to promote COVID-19 vaccinations among young people. She even met with President Joe Biden, Vice President Kamala Harris, and Dr. Anthony Fauci to discuss the importance of vaccination. Olivia recorded videos and posted on social media to encourage her fans to get the shot, using her platform to help keep people safe during the pandemic. Not every day you see a pop star working with the President of the United States! Olivia's involvement showed that she's not just a talented artist-she's also someone who cares deeply about making a positive impact.

30: Olivia's ASCAP Songwriter of the Year Award- Twice!

Winning Songwriter of the Year is a huge achievement, and Olivia did it twice! In 2022 and 2024, Olivia was named ASCAP's Songwriter of the Year, an award that celebrates her incredible talent for writing meaningful, relatable songs. It's rare for an artist to win such a prestigious award early in their career. Still, Olivia's ability to craft powerful lyrics has made her stand out in the music world. Being recognized for her songwriting proves that she's more than just a pop star-she's an artist who connects with people through her words.

Show Off Your Olivia Smarts!

5. What city was Olivia born?

    A) Los Angeles
    B) Sacramento
    C) Murrieta
    D) San Francisco

6. What color dress does Olivia wear in the "Drivers License" music video?

    A) Red
    B) White
    C) Blue
    D) Black

Did you know?

31: Olivia's First-Ever Concert

Do you remember your first concert? For Olivia, it was seeing one of her biggest musical inspirations live in concert-Taylor Swift! Olivia has often talked about how much she loves Taylor's music and how seeing her perform greatly impacted her. It's easy to see how Taylor's influence helped shape Olivia's style as a singer and songwriter. Who knows, maybe one day Olivia will be the artist inspiring future generations at their first concerts! If you've ever been to a live show, you know that nothing beats the feeling of hearing your favorite songs in person.

32: Olivia's Favorite Snack-Takis!

You've heard of Olivia's love for music and acting, but here's a fun fact you might not know: Olivia's favorite snack is Takis! These spicy rolled tortilla chips are known for their bold flavor, and Olivia has said she can't get enough of them. Whether she's on tour, in the studio, or just chilling at home, Takis are Olivia's go-to treat. It's always fun to learn what our favorite stars snack on, isn't it? Next time you're munching on a bag of Takis, you can think of Olivia and know you're sharing the same spicy snack!

33: Olivia's Record-Breaking First Week on Spotify

We all know that Olivia's hit song "Drivers License" took the world by storm, but did you know it broke not one but two Spotify records in its first week? The song set the record for the most streams in a single day by a non-holiday song, with over 17 million streams. It didn't stop there-by the end of the week, "Drivers License" had also become the first song in history to reach over 80 million streams in just seven days! That's a lot of people listening to Olivia pour her heart out. Have you ever listened to a song on repeat like that?

34: Olivia's Role in the "She Can STEM" Campaign

In 2018, Olivia joined the "She Can STEM" campaign, encouraging girls to pursue science, technology, engineering, and math careers. Olivia worked with the campaign to inspire young girls to believe that they can do anything they set their minds to-even in traditionally male-dominated fields. It's amazing to see Olivia using her platform to empower young girls to follow their passions, whether it's in music, acting, or STEM. Olivia is cheering you on if you're ever thinking about a future in science or technology!

35: Olivia's Favorite Subject in School Was English

Even though Olivia became a superstar at a young age, she's always been a fan of learning. One of her favorite subjects in school was English, which makes sense when you think about her songwriting skills! Olivia has always loved reading and writing, which has clearly helped her craft the powerful lyrics she's known for today. Her passion for English gave her a strong foundation in storytelling, something that shines through in every song she writes. If you enjoy English class, you're in good company-Olivia loves it too!

36: Olivia's Collaboration with Casetify

Olivia's creativity goes beyond just music-she has a flair for design! In December 2021, Olivia teamed up with Casetify, a phone accessory company, to create her very own line of phone cases. Inspired by her debut album Sour, Olivia's "Hardened Hearts" collection featured bold designs with a cool, 90s-inspired vibe. Fans loved how Olivia's personal style came through in the phone cases, making it a fun and unique collaboration. Do you have a favorite phone case that shows off your personality, just like Olivia's designs?

Did you know?

37: Olivia's Friendship with Madison Hu

Friendships made on set are often some of the strongest, and that's definitely the case for Olivia and her Bizaardvark co-star Madison Hu. The two actresses became best friends while filming the Disney Channel show, and they've stayed close ever since. Olivia and Madison often post about each other on social media, showing fans how strong their bond is. It's heartwarming to see how their friendship has lasted even after the show ended. Do you have a best friend who's always by your side, no matter what?

38: Olivia's Support for Women in Music

As a young woman in the music industry, Olivia knows firsthand how important it is to support other women. That's why she's been vocal about celebrating female artists and making sure women's voices are heard in the industry. Olivia often talks about how much she admires trailblazing women like Taylor Swift, Lorde, and Alanis Morissette, and she hopes to inspire the next generation of female musicians. It's awesome to see Olivia using her success to lift up other women in music. Who's a female artist that inspires you?

Did you know?

39: Olivia's Vinyl-Exclusive EP

Here's a cool fact for vinyl collectors-Olivia released a special vinyl-exclusive EP in 2023! She dropped Guts: The Secret Tracks to celebrate Record Store Day, featuring four previously unreleased songs that fans could only get on vinyl. The limited-edition release quickly became one of the top sellers during Record Store Day, showing that Olivia's fans are always eager to hear new music from her. Vinyl records have made a huge comeback recently, and Olivia's exclusive EP gave fans another reason to love collecting them. Do you have any favorite albums on vinyl?

40: Olivia's Acting Coach Made a Big Impact

Before Olivia became a household name, her acting coach, Jennifer Dustman, played a huge role in shaping her talent. Olivia started working with Dustman when she was just a kid, and it was under her guidance that Olivia's parents enrolled her in various local singing competitions and acting lessons. Jennifer encouraged Olivia to pursue her dreams, and her mentorship had a big impact on Olivia's journey. Sometimes, all it takes is one person who believes in you to help you reach your full potential. Has there ever been someone in your life who helped you achieve your goals?

41: Olivia's Love for Journaling

Did you know that Olivia loves to journal? She's said that keeping a journal is one of her favorite ways to express her thoughts and emotions, which probably explains why her lyrics feel so personal and relatable. Olivia often writes about her feelings in her journal, which inspires her to write songs. Journaling helps her process her emotions and turn them into music that connects with fans worldwide. If you've ever kept a journal, you know how powerful it can be to put your thoughts on paper. Have you ever tried journaling like Olivia?

42: Olivia's Family Keeps Her Grounded

Even though Olivia's life has changed dramatically since becoming a global superstar, her family plays a big role in keeping her grounded. Olivia has often said how close she is with her parents, Jennifer and Chris, and how much she appreciates their support throughout her career. Her parents have been by her side from the beginning, and Olivia credits them with helping her stay true to herself, even as her fame skyrocketed. It's clear that family means a lot to Olivia, and it's a big reason she's been able to navigate her career with grace and humility. Isn't it amazing how family can be such a strong support system?

Show Off Your Olivia Smarts!

7. Which song on *Sour* almost didn't make it onto the album?

A) Jealousy, Jealousy
B) Favorite Crime
C) Brutal
D) 1 Step Forward, 3 Steps Back

8. What is Olivia Rodrigo's middle name?

A) Grace
B) Isabel
C) Marie
D) Sophia

Did you know?

43: Olivia's Favorite Book Is The Catcher in the Rye

In interviews, Olivia shared that one of her favorite books is The Catcher in the Rye by J.D. Salinger. The classic novel, which tells the story of a teenager struggling to find his place in the world, resonates with Olivia because of its themes of growing up and self-discovery. It's no wonder she connects with it, considering that much of her own music reflects the emotional ups and downs of being a teenager. If you're a fan of literature, this is a book you'll enjoy reading, too! Have you ever read The Catcher in the Rye?

44: Olivia's Songwriting are inspired from Real Life

One of the reasons Olivia's songs feel so personal is because they're inspired by her own experiences. Whether writing about heartbreak, friendship, or the challenges of growing up, Olivia draws from real-life events to create music that connects her fans. She's often said that songwriting helps her process her emotions, turning tough moments into something beautiful. That's why her lyrics feel so relatable-because they come from the heart. Have you ever listened to one of Olivia's songs and thought, "Wow, that's exactly how I feel!"?

45: Olivia's Acting Debut at 7 Years Old

Olivia's career started early-she made her acting debut at just 7!
She appeared in a commercial for Old Navy, her first experience
in front of the camera. Even though it was a small role, it
marked the beginning of a career that would eventually lead to
Disney Channel stardom and international fame. Amazingly,
Olivia started her journey in showbiz at a young age. Still, even
then, it was clear she had something special. Can you imagine
starting your career before you even hit double digits?

46: Olivia's Close Friendship with Jenna Ortega

Did you know that Olivia is friends with Wednesday star Jenna
Ortega? The two rising stars have bonded over their
experiences in the entertainment industry and often support
each other's careers. Fans love seeing their friendship, as Olivia
and Jenna are known for their authenticity and down-to-earth
personalities. Their connection is a great reminder that even in
the fast-paced world of Hollywood, true friendships can still
thrive. Have you ever had a friend who always has your back,
just like Olivia and Jenna do for each other?

Did you know?

47: Olivia's Connection to Lorde's Music

Olivia has often mentioned how much she admires the New Zealand singer-songwriter Lorde. In fact, some critics have compared Olivia's introspective songwriting to Lorde's, especially in how both artists explore complex emotions in their music. Lorde's influence can be heard in the moody, atmospheric vibes of Olivia's songs like "Deja Vu" and "Traitor." It's cool to see how Olivia's musical inspirations helped shape her unique sound while allowing her to put her own spin on things. Have you noticed any Lorde-like vibes in Olivia's music?

48: Olivia Graduated High School While Filming Sour

Balancing a skyrocketing career with schoolwork is challenging. Still, Olivia managed to graduate high school while working on her debut album, Sour. She was homeschooled during her final years of high school, which allowed her to focus on her music while still finishing her education. It's pretty impressive that she was able to juggle both at the same time! Olivia's hard work paid off, as she earned her diploma in 2021-the same year she released Sour and became a global sensation. Have you ever balanced school with a big project like Olivia did?

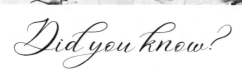
Did you know?

49: Olivia's Song "Vampire" Set New Records

When Olivia released her song "Vampire" in 2023, it quickly became another record-breaker for her. The song debuted at number one on the Billboard Hot 100, making Olivia the first artist to debut the lead singles from two albums at number one on the chart. "Vampire" is a powerful track about feeling betrayed, and it showcases Olivia's ability to turn raw emotions into a hit song. Fans immediately connected with the song's intensity, which solidified Olivia's place as one of the most exciting young artists in pop music today. Have you heard "Vampire" yet? It's a must-listen!

50: Olivia's Early Love for Taylor Swift's Fearless

Olivia has been a huge fan of Taylor Swift for as long as she can remember, and one of the albums that had the biggest impact on her was Fearless. Released in 2008, Fearless was the album that inspired Olivia to start writing her own songs. She was especially drawn to Taylor's honest lyrics and storytelling, which helped shape Olivia's own approach to songwriting. It's no surprise that Taylor is one of Olivia's biggest musical influences, and Olivia has said that hearing Fearless made her believe she could write songs that meant something to people. What's an album that inspires you like Fearless inspired Olivia?

51: Olivia Was Named Billboard's Woman of the Year in 2022

In 2022, Olivia was honored with Billboard's prestigious Woman of the Year award. This title recognizes her incredible impact on the music industry. This award is given to artists who have achieved major success and made a difference in the world of music. At just 19 years old, Olivia was the youngest recipient of the award, proving that her influence extends far beyond her age. It was a huge moment in her career, showing how quickly she became a major pop culture force. Can you imagine winning such a big award at such a young age?

52: Olivia's Fun Collection of Stickers

Here's a fun and quirky fact-Olivia loves stickers! In interviews, she mentioned that she has a pretty impressive collection of them. From colorful, glittery ones to unique designs, stickers are one of her favorite things to collect. She even designed some fun, bold stickers to go along with the Sour album merch! Olivia's playful side comes out in her love for these tiny, decorative pieces, and it's a hobby that her fans can definitely relate to. Do you have a favorite collection like Olivia's stickers?

Did you know?

53: Olivia's Hidden Talent-Baking!

When she's not writing songs or performing, Olivia enjoys baking as a fun way to relax and express her creativity. One of her specialties is cookies, and she's shared how much she loves experimenting with different recipes in the kitchen. Baking is a hobby that allows her to step away from the busy world of music and unwind, which is something we all need from time to time! Whether whipping up a batch of cookies or trying out new desserts, Olivia's love for baking shows she has skills beyond the stage. Do you have a favorite treat to bake?

54: Olivia's Love for Classic Movies

Olivia isn't just a music fan-she's also a big fan of classic movies. She mentioned in interviews that she loves watching old films, especially those from the 1950s and '60s. Movies like Breakfast at Tiffany's and Rebel Without a Cause are some of her favorites, and she draws inspiration from the timeless style and storytelling in these films. It's pretty cool how Olivia's love for classic cinema influences her aesthetic and creative vision. Do you enjoy classic movies? If so, you've got something in common with Olivia!

Show Off Your Olivia Smarts!

9. What was Olivia's first acting role in a Disney Channel show?

A) Andi Mack
B) Bizaardvark
C) Liv and Maddie
D) Jessie

10. What iconic band did Olivia perform with at Coachella in 2024?

A) Pearl Jam
B) Green Day
C) No Doubt
D) Paramore

Did you know?

55: Olivia's Sour Album Was Recorded During the Pandemic

Did you know that Olivia recorded most of Sour during the COVID-19 pandemic? While the world was on lockdown, Olivia worked on her debut album with producer Dan Nigro, often recording from her own home. The pandemic presented unique challenges but also gave Olivia time to reflect and create some of her most personal and emotional songs. The result? An album that resonated with millions of listeners who were going through their own emotional journeys during that time. Isn't it amazing how something so impactful can emerge from such difficult circumstances?

56: Olivia's Influence on Gen Z Fashion

Olivia has become a major style icon for Gen Z, influencing fashion trends with her fun and edgy looks. From her Sour album cover outfits to her red-carpet appearances, Olivia's style is all about mixing playful, retro pieces with modern touches. She's known for rocking bold colors, unique patterns, and a mix of high and low fashion that fans love to copy. Whether she's wearing chunky boots or colorful skirts, Olivia's fashion choices have made her one of the most-watched young style stars today. Have you ever been inspired by one of Olivia's outfits?

57: Olivia's Impact on Streaming Platforms

Not only did Olivia break records on Spotify, but she also had a huge impact on Apple Music and YouTube. Her music videos for songs like "Drivers License" and "Good 4 U" quickly racked up millions of views, and her songs dominated streaming charts worldwide. In fact, her debut album, Sour, was the most-streamed album of 2021 on both Spotify and Apple Music. Olivia's music resonated with listeners across every platform, proving her talent and storytelling reached far and wide. Have you ever binge-watched her music videos on YouTube?

58: Olivia's Collaboration with Sony on Special Edition Earbuds

In 2023, Olivia teamed up with Sony to release their Linkbuds S earbuds in a special edition. Inspired by her Sour album, these earbuds were designed to celebrate her musical journey while offering high-quality sound for fans. It was a fun collaboration that gave fans a unique way to listen to Olivia's music while rocking a piece of her personal style. The limited-edition earbuds were a hit, showing that Olivia's influence extends beyond just music-she's also making waves in the tech world. Wouldn't it be cool to listen to Sour on earbuds designed by Olivia herself?

Did you know?

59: Olivia's Big Love for Converse Sneakers

If you're a fan of Olivia's fashion, you might have noticed that she's often seen rocking a pair of classic Converse sneakers. Whether out and about or performing on stage, Olivia loves to pair her outfits with Converse shoes, giving her a cool, laid-back vibe. Converse sneakers have been a staple in Olivia's wardrobe for years, and she's worn them with everything from casual jeans to more dressed-up outfits. It's a style choice that fans love to copy, and it's easy to see why-Converse goes with just about anything! Do you have a favorite pair of sneakers that you wear all the time?

60: Olivia Once Dreamed of Becoming a Veterinarian

Before she became a global music sensation, Olivia had a completely different career dream-she wanted to be a veterinarian! Growing up, Olivia loved animals and thought working with them as a vet would be amazing. While her path ultimately led her to music and acting, her love for animals never faded. In fact, Olivia has said that if she weren't an artist, being a vet would still be high on her list of dream jobs. It's always fun to learn about what our favorite stars wanted to be when they were younger, isn't it? Do you have a dream job that's totally different from what you're doing now?

Did you know?

61: Olivia's First Grammy Award Show Experience

Attending the Grammy Awards is a big deal for any artist. Olivia's first experience at the Grammys in 2022 was unforgettable. Not only did she attend the event, but she also performed live and took home three awards! It was a whirlwind night filled with excitement, and fans were thrilled to see Olivia shining on one of the biggest stages in music. Olivia's Grammy performance and wins marked a major milestone in her career, showing the world that she's not just a rising star-she's a force to be reckoned with. Can you imagine performing at such a legendary event?

62: Olivia's Support for Mental Health Awareness

Olivia has been open about the importance of mental health, and she often uses her platform to support mental health awareness. She's spoken in interviews about her own struggles with anxiety and the pressures of fame, encouraging her fans to prioritize their mental well-being. Olivia's music also touches on themes of mental health, with songs like "Brutal" and "Traitor" reflecting the emotional challenges of growing up. By being honest about her own experiences, Olivia has become an advocate for mental health, inspiring her fans to care for themselves, too. It's refreshing to see someone in the spotlight talk about such an important issue, don't you think?

Did you know?

63: Olivia's Appearance in High School Musical Was Almost Different

Can you imagine Olivia playing a different character in High School Musical: The Musical: The Series? It almost happened! Originally, Olivia auditioned for the role of Gina Porter, but she ended up being cast as Nini Salazar-Roberts instead. The switch was the perfect fit for Olivia, as her character, Nini, quickly became a fan favorite. It's always interesting to think about how things could have turned out differently, but in this case, it seems like everything worked out just right! Have you ever been in a situation where a change ended up being the best thing for you?

64: Olivia's Admiration for Cardi B

While Olivia's music has a more emotional, introspective vibe, she's a big fan of Cardi B's bold, confident style. Olivia has mentioned in interviews how much she admires Cardi's fearlessness and how she owns her personality, both in her music and real life. Olivia even tweeted that she was "crying" when Cardi praised Sour on social media! It's always fun to see artists from different genres supporting each other, and it's clear that Olivia looks up to Cardi for her unapologetic attitude. Who's an artist that inspires you to be more confident and fearless?

65: Olivia's Favorite Disney Character

Here's a fun fact-Olivia's favorite Disney character is Ariel from The Little Mermaid! In interviews, She mentioned that she's always loved Ariel's adventurous spirit and willingness to follow her dreams, even when it meant leaving her comfort zone. It's easy to see why Olivia relates to the character, as Ariel and Olivia have shown bravery in going after what they want. Whether you're a fan of the classic Disney princesses or the newer ones, something is inspiring about characters who chase their dreams, just like Olivia has done in her own life. Who's your favorite Disney character?

66: Olivia's Successful Sour Tour Merchandise

Fans love Olivia's music, but they also love her merch! When Olivia launched her Sour Tour in 2022, she released a line of tour merchandise that sold out quickly. From T-shirts and hoodies to posters and accessories, Olivia's merch was a hit with fans who wanted a piece of her tour experience. The Sour merch had a cool, edgy aesthetic that reflected the album's vibe, making it a must-have for Olivia's biggest supporters. Merchandise is one of the many ways fans can feel connected to their favorite artists. Olivia's fans showed their love by grabbing the items as fast as possible. Do you own any cool merch from your favorite artists?

11. Which song on Sour features an interpolation of a Taylor Swift song?

A) Jealousy, Jealousy
B) 1 Step Forward, 3 Steps Back
C) Deja Vu
D) Happier

12. In what year did Olivia start playing guitar?

A) 9
B) 10
C) 12
D) 14

Did you know?

67: Olivia's Passion for Environmental Causes

Olivia cares deeply about the environment and has used her platform to raise awareness about climate change. She's been vocal about the importance of protecting the planet and has encouraged her fans to take action in their own communities. Olivia has even participated in Earth Day campaigns, using her influence to highlight the need for sustainability and environmental responsibility. It's inspiring to see a young artist who is focused on her music and making the world a better place. Do you do anything to help protect the environment, like recycling or reducing plastic use?

68: Olivia's Love for Vintage Cars

Here's a fun fact: Olivia loves vintage cars! She's mentioned in interviews how much she admires the style and design of classic cars, and she even got to drive one in the music video for "Drivers License." That scene, with Olivia behind the wheel of a vintage car, perfectly captured the nostalgic, emotional feeling of the song. While she might not own a vintage vehicle herself just yet, it's clear that Olivia's appreciation for timeless style extends beyond just fashion and music. What's your favorite kind of car-classic or modern?

Did you know?

69: Olivia's Dedication to Female Empowerment

Throughout her career, Olivia has been a strong advocate for female empowerment. She's often spoken about how important it is for women to lift each other up, especially in industries like music, where female voices haven't always been heard. Olivia's songs, like "Brutal" and "Good 4 U," have become anthems for young women, encouraging them to embrace their strength and independence. By sharing her own experiences and struggles, Olivia is helping create a space where girls and women can feel empowered to be themselves. Who's a woman in your life who inspires you to be strong?

70: Olivia's Appearance on Saturday Night Live

One of Olivia's biggest career highlights was her performance on Saturday Night Live (SNL) in 2021. It was a huge moment for her, as SNL is known for featuring some of the biggest musical acts in the world. Olivia performed her hits "Drivers License" and "Good 4 U" on the show, wowing the audience with her powerful vocals and emotional delivery. The appearance helped cement her status as a rising star, and fans loved seeing her bring her songs to life on such an iconic stage. Have you ever watched a performance on SNL that gave you chills?

71: Olivia's Creative Writing Background

Before Olivia became a famous singer-songwriter, she had a strong interest in creative writing. Even as a child, she would write stories and poems, which later helped her develop her songwriting skills. Olivia has said that writing has always been a way for her to express her emotions and that her passion for storytelling comes through in her music today. Olivia's creativity shines through, whether writing a song or crafting a poem. Do you enjoy writing stories or poems like Olivia does?

72: Olivia's Role in Promoting Education for Girls

In 2021, Olivia launched her "Spicy Pisces T-shirts" campaign, with all proceeds going to the nonprofit organization She's the First. The organization focuses on providing scholarships and education opportunities for girls worldwide. Olivia's dedication to supporting girls' education is just one example of how she uses her fame for good. She believes in the power of education to change lives, and her fans were eager to support the cause by purchasing her limited-edition shirts. Seeing someone so young make such a big impact on the world is amazing. Have you ever supported a reason you're passionate about?

73: Olivia's Unique Approach to Songwriting

When it comes to songwriting, Olivia has a unique approach. She's shared that she often writes lyrics before coming up with the melody, focusing first on the emotions she wants to express. For Olivia, the words are the heart of the song, and once she has the lyrics down, she works on creating music that complements the feelings behind them. This method has helped her craft songs that resonate deeply with listeners, as the lyrics are always raw, honest, and emotional. Do you ever write your feelings down before turning them into something creative?

74: Olivia's Connection to Avril Lavigne

Olivia has often cited Avril Lavigne as one of her biggest musical inspirations. Growing up, Olivia was a huge fan of Avril's music, especially her early hits like "Complicated" and "Sk8er Boi." The influence of Avril's edgy, rebellious style can be heard in some of Olivia's own songs, like "Good 4 U," which has a pop-punk vibe that's reminiscent of Avril's sound. In 2022, Olivia met Avril in person, and the two shared a moment that was a dream come true for Olivia. Isn't it amazing to meet someone who's inspired you for so long?

Did you know?

75: Olivia's Acoustic Performances Are Magical

While Olivia is known for her high-energy performances and bold pop-rock sound, she's also amazing when performing acoustically. Stripping her songs to just her voice and a guitar or piano shows her raw talent and emotional depth. Fans especially love her acoustic versions of hits like "Drivers License" and "Traitor," where Olivia's voice shines, and the lyrics feel even more powerful. It's in these intimate performances that Olivia's connection with her audience truly stands out. Have you ever watched an acoustic performance that gave you goosebumps?

76: Olivia's Style Icon is Gwen Stefani

Olivia often mentions that she looks up to Gwen Stefani as a major style icon. Gwen's fearless fashion choices, from her punk-rock looks in the '90s to her bold, glamorous outfits today, have inspired Olivia to experiment with her own style. Like Gwen, Olivia isn't afraid to mix edgy and feminine pieces, creating a look that's all her own. Olivia's ability to take fashion risks while staying true to herself makes her a standout style star for her generation. Have you ever been inspired by a celebrity's fashion choices?

Did you know?

77: Olivia Has a Favorite Song from Sour

Of all the amazing songs on her debut album Sour, Olivia has revealed that one of her favorites is "Favorite Crime." The song is a fan favorite, too, thanks to its haunting melody and vulnerable lyrics. Olivia has said that she loves how emotional and bittersweet the song feels, capturing the pain and regret of a difficult relationship. It's always interesting to hear which songs mean the most to artists, especially when they come from such a personal place. Do you have a favorite song from Sour?

78: Olivia's Zodiac Sign is Pisces

Born on February 20, 2003, Olivia is a Pisces, and many fans think her zodiac sign matches her personality perfectly. Pisces is known for being creative, sensitive, and empathetic, all qualities that come through in Olivia's music and songwriting. Her ability to tap into deep emotions and express them in such a relatable way is a classic Pisces trait. Olivia even launched a line of "Spicy Pisces" T-shirts as a fun nod to her star sign! Do you know your zodiac sign and what it says about your personality?

Show Off Your Olivia Smarts!

13. What major record label did Olivia sign with to release her music?

A) Capitol Records
B) Geffen Records
C) RCA Records
D) Columbia Records

14. How many Grammy Awards did Olivia win in 2022?

A) 1
B) 2
C) 3
D) 4

79: Olivia Wrote Sour in Her Bedroom

While some artists write their songs in fancy studios, Olivia wrote much of Sour in her own bedroom. During the pandemic, Olivia had a lot of time to reflect and poured her thoughts and feelings into her songwriting. The result was a deeply personal album that captured the ups and downs of young adulthood, love, and heartbreak. Writing in the comfort of her own space allowed Olivia to be as honest as possible, and that authenticity is one of the reasons Sour resonated so strongly with fans. Isn't it inspiring to think you can create something amazing from your room?

80: Olivia's Global Philanthropic Efforts

Olivia's desire to help others goes beyond her local community. In 2023, she expanded her philanthropic efforts to a global scale by supporting international organizations like Women Against Violence Europe. Olivia believes in using her platform to help women and girls worldwide, especially when facing challenges like violence and limited access to education. Her dedication to making the world a better place for women everywhere is another reason fans admire her. Have you ever been involved in a cause that helps others globally?

81: Olivia's Inspiration for "Good 4 U"

When Olivia wrote "Good 4 U," she wanted to create a song that captured the fiery emotions of a breakup but with a rock edge. She drew inspiration from the pop-punk bands she grew up listening to, like Paramore and Green Day. The song's rebellious energy and Olivia's sharp lyrics made it an instant hit. Fans loved how it mixed anger with empowerment, creating a breakup anthem perfect for blasting at full volume. Who doesn't love a good breakup anthem that makes you feel strong and confident?

82: Olivia's Artistic Collaboration with Other Young Stars

Olivia has built strong connections with other young artists in the industry, including Conan Gray and Joshua Bassett. These friendships have become artistic collaborations fans love, as the artists support each other's music and careers. Olivia and Conan often tease the idea of working on a song together, and fans are eager to see what kind of magic they could create. Collaborations between artists who truly admire each other often lead to amazing music. Is there a dream collaboration you'd love to see Olivia be part of?

83: Olivia Was Time's Entertainer of the Year in 2021

In 2021, Olivia was named Time magazine's entertainer of the year-a huge honor recognizing her incredible impact on music and pop culture in such a short time. This award celebrated her breakout success with Sour and her ability to connect with fans worldwide through her emotionally charged lyrics. It was a major moment in Olivia's career, showing how quickly she became a global icon. Imagine being named the top entertainer of the year when you're only 18! That's Olivia's power.

84: Olivia Loves a Good Board Game Night

Even though Olivia's life is filled with music and performances, she still enjoys kicking back with her friends and family for a good board game night. Whether it's a classic game like Monopoly or something a little more modern, Olivia loves the fun and laughter that comes from spending time playing games with her loved ones. It's a reminder that no matter how busy life gets, relaxing and enjoying some good, old-fashioned fun is always nice. Do you have a favorite board game you love playing with friends?

85: Olivia Has a Soft Spot for Dogs

Olivia is a huge animal lover and is especially fond of dogs. She's mentioned how much she adores spending time with furry friends and even said that one of her dream pets is a rescue dog. Many of Olivia's fans can relate to her love for animals, especially dogs, as there's nothing quite like the bond between a person and their pet. If you're an animal lover like Olivia, you know how special that connection can be. Do you have a pet, or is there a certain kind of animal you dream of having one day?

86: Olivia's Songs Are Part of TikTok Culture

Olivia's music isn't just popular on the charts-it's also a huge hit on TikTok! Songs like "Drivers License" and "Good 4 U" have been used in countless TikTok videos, with fans creating everything from emotional montages to dance routines inspired by her music. TikTok played a big role in spreading Olivia's songs to an even wider audience, and it's one of the reasons her music has become a cultural phenomenon. If you've ever spent time on TikTok, chances are you've come across a video with one of Olivia's songs in the background!

Did you know?

87: Olivia's Handwritten Lyrics Are a Fan Favorite

One of the coolest things about Olivia is how connected she is to her fans. As a special treat, she's shared handwritten versions of her song lyrics on social media, giving fans a peek into her creative process. The handwritten lyrics, complete with little doodles and notes, have become a fan favorite, as they offer a personal and intimate look at how Olivia's songs come together. It's a reminder that behind the superstar is an artist who pours her heart into every word. Have you ever written something out by hand that felt more special than typing it out?

88: Olivia's Collaboration with Health-Ade

In 2023, Olivia teamed up with Health-Ade to launch a special smoothie called "Good 4 Ur Guts" (a fun nod to her hit song "Good 4 U"). The smoothie was a limited edition available at Erewhon Market stores and featured healthy, gut-friendly ingredients. It was another example of how Olivia expanded her influence beyond music, using her platform to promote wellness and self-care. Fans loved grabbing a healthy treat inspired by Olivia's music! Wouldn't it be cool to try a drink inspired by one of your favorite songs?

89: Olivia's Favorite Ice Cream Flavor Is Mint Chocolate Chip

Who doesn't love ice cream? Olivia's go-to flavor is mint chocolate chip, a refreshing choice that mixes cool mint with sweet chocolate chunks. It's the perfect dessert for someone like Olivia, who loves a mix of classic and bold flavors. Whether she's grabbing a scoop after a long day or celebrating a career milestone, mint chocolate chip is her favorite sweet treat. What's your favorite ice cream flavor, and does it match up with Olivia's?

90: Olivia's "Deja Vu" Was Inspired by TV Shows

The idea for Olivia's hit song "Deja Vu" came from her love of watching TV shows with friends. She mentioned in interviews that the song reflects the feeling of doing something special with someone, only to later see them doing the same thing with someone else-just like when you watch a favorite show with one person, and then they start watching it with someone new. The clever concept of "Deja Vu" combined with Olivia's sharp lyrics made the song an instant hit. Do you have a favorite show that you love to watch over and over again?

Show Off Your Olivia Smarts!

15. What was the name of the prom-themed concert film Olivia released in 2021?

A) Sour Prom
B) Prom Queen
C) Prom Night
D) High School Prom

16. Which artist is a major influence on Olivia's pop-punk sound in songs like "Good 4 U"?

A) Taylor Swift
B) Avril Lavigne
C) Billie Eilish
D) Cardi B

89: Olivia's Favorite Place to Write Songs Is by the Ocean

When Olivia needs inspiration for songwriting, one of her favorite places to go is by the ocean. She's shared how the calmness of the water helps her clear her mind and focus on her music. The ocean's beauty and tranquility often provide the perfect backdrop for her to explore her feelings and turn them into powerful lyrics. Whether it's the sound of the waves or the fresh air, something about being near the water helps Olivia tap into her creativity. Do you have a favorite place that sparks your creativity?

90: Olivia's Emotional Songwriting Is Inspired by Journaling

For Olivia, songwriting is a lot like keeping a diary. She's said that writing down her thoughts and feelings in a journal helps her turn them into song lyrics. That's why her music feels so personal-because it often comes straight from her journal entries! This raw honesty is what fans love most about Olivia's music, as it feels like she's letting them into her world with each song. If you've ever kept a journal, you know how powerful it can be to express your emotions through writing. Have you ever turned your journal entries into something creative?

Did you know?

91: Olivia's Dream Collaboration Is with Jack White

One of Olivia's dream collaborations is with Jack White, the legendary rock musician from The White Stripes. She's called him her "hero of all heroes" and admires his ability to blend rock with emotional storytelling. Olivia has mentioned how much she'd love to work with Jack someday, combining his raw, electric sound with her own style of songwriting. While they haven't teamed up yet, fans eagerly await to see if this dream collaboration will ever happen. Can you imagine the kind of music they would make together?

Fact: 92: Olivia's Favorite Movie Genre Is Horror

While Olivia is known for her emotional, heartfelt songs, her favorite movie genre might surprise you-she loves horror films! Olivia has mentioned that she enjoys watching scary movies, especially with friends. The thrill of a good horror flick helps her unwind after a long day, even if it means getting a few jump scares along the way. Whether it's classic horror or new releases, Olivia enjoys the adrenaline rush of a good scare. Are you brave enough to watch horror movies like Olivia?

Fact: 93: Olivia Wrote a Christmas Song at Age Five

Most people are learning how to write letters at age five, but Olivia was already writing songs! When she was just a kindergartener, she wrote her first-ever song called "The Bels"- a Christmas tune that's both adorable and catchy. Olivia shared a snippet of it on social media, and fans loved hearing this early glimpse into her musical talent. It's pretty amazing that Olivia was writing songs before most kids even read chapter books! Can you imagine writing a song when you were in kindergarten?

Fact: 94: Olivia Loves Collecting Vinyl Records

Olivia has a love for music that goes beyond streaming platforms-she's also a huge fan of vinyl records. Olivia enjoys collecting records from some of her favorite artists, especially older albums with a timeless sound. She's said that listening to music on vinyl gives her a deeper connection to the music, as the sound quality and experience of playing records are different from digital formats. Olivia's love for vinyl shows that she appreciates music in all its forms. Do you have a favorite way to listen to music?

Fact 95: Olivia's Song "Brutal" Almost Didn't Make It on Sour

One of Olivia's most popular songs, "Brutal," almost didn't make it onto her debut album, Sour. The song's raw energy and punk rock vibe made it stand out from the rest of the album, and Olivia wasn't sure if it fit with the overall sound. However, she decided to include it after some back-and-forth, and fans were so glad she did! "Brutal" quickly became a fan favorite and showed a different side of Olivia's musical abilities. Sometimes, taking a risk can pay off in a big way. Have you ever almost given up on something, only to be glad you didn't?

Fact 96: Olivia Taught Herself to Play Guitar

Olivia didn't take formal guitar lessons-she taught herself to play! At age 12, she picked up the instrument. She started learning independently by watching YouTube tutorials and practicing with her favorite songs. Her love for music motivated her to keep practicing until she mastered it, and now she uses the guitar to write many of her songs. It's proof that if you're passionate about something, you can learn a lot on your own. Do you play any instruments, or is there one you'd love to learn?

Fact 97: Olivia's Vintage Fashion Inspiration Comes from the '90s

Olivia's unique sense of style is often inspired by the fashion of the 1990s. From oversized blazers and platform shoes to plaid skirts and grunge looks, Olivia loves experimenting with throwback trends that give her outfits a cool, retro vibe. She often wears clothes that mix vintage pieces with modern twists, making her style stand out best. Olivia's love for '90s fashion shows that she has a creative approach to her personal style. What's your favorite fashion era?

Fact 98: Olivia Once Performed at the White House

In 2021, Olivia visited the White House to help promote COVID-19 vaccinations among young people. She met with President Joe Biden and Vice President Kamala Harris as part of the effort. She even performed a few songs to encourage youth to get vaccinated. Olivia's White House visit showed her commitment to using her platform for good causes, and it was a big honor for someone so young to be involved in such an important initiative. How cool would it be to perform at the White House?

Did you know?

Fact 99: Olivia's First Job for the Old Navy

Before she was a Disney star and music sensation, Olivia's very first acting job was in a commercial for Old Navy. She was just 7 years old when she appeared in the commercial, which marked the beginning of her career in front of the camera. Although it was a small role, it helped launch Olivia into the world of acting, and the rest is history! It's fun to think that even the biggest stars often start with small roles. Have you ever had a first job that helped you reach your goals?

Fact 100: Olivia's Hidden Talent Is Knitting

While most fans know Olivia for her musical talents, she has another hobby that might surprise you-knitting! Olivia enjoys knitting to relax and take her mind off the fast-paced world of music. She does it during her downtime, and she's even made scarves and other items for friends and family. Knitting might not be as well-known as her music, but it's a talent that shows her creative side in a new way. Have you ever tried knitting or making something by hand?

Show Off Your Olivia Smarts!

17. What is Olivia's favorite ice cream flavor?

A) Chocolate
B) Strawberry
C) Mint Chocolate Chip
D) Vanilla

18. Which song of Olivia's was featured on the soundtrack for The Hunger Games: The Ballad of Songbirds & Snakes?

A) Deja Vu
B) Can't Catch Me Now
C) Jealousy, Jealousy
D) Brutal

19. What year did Olivia first appear in a commercial for Old Navy?

A) 2007
B) 2009
C) 2010
D) 2012

20. How many Billboard Hot 100 number-one singles does Olivia have as of 2023?

A) 1
B) 2
C) 3
D) 4

Extended Trivia!

21. What song did Olivia release as the lead single from her album Guts in 2023?

A) Vampire
B) Bad Idea Right?
C) Favorite Crime
D) Deja Vu

22. Who did Olivia dedicate her 2022 Grammy wins to?

A) Her fans
B) Her parents
C) Her acting coach
D) Her songwriting idols

23. Which high school did Olivia attend before being homeschooled?

A) Dorothy McElhinney Middle School
B) Temecula High School
C) Santa Monica High School
D) Lisa J. Mails Elementary

Extended Trivia!

24. What song from Sour became a viral TikTok trend for its catchy chorus?

A) Traitor
B) Jealousy, Jealousy
C) Brutal
D) Good 4 U

25. Olivia's debut album, Sour, spent how many weeks at number one on the Billboard 200 chart?

A) 1 week
B) 3 weeks
C) 5 weeks
D) 7 weeks

26. Who inspired Olivia to start writing songs after hearing Fearless?

A) Taylor Swift
B) Lorde
C) Billie Eilish
D) Lana Del Rey

Extended Trivia!

27. What school activity did Olivia participate in that helped spark her love for performing?

A) Choir
B) Musical Theater Program
C) Debate Club
D) Dance Team

28. How old was Olivia when she started songwriting?

A) 10
B) 11
C) 12
D) 13

29. What does Olivia consider her favorite song on Guts?

A) Vampire
B) Lacy
C) Get Him Back!
D) Love is Embarrassing

Extended Trivia!

30. Olivia's song "Drivers License" broke which of the following streaming records?

A) Most streams in a single day on Spotify
B) Fastest song to reach 1 billion streams
C) First debut single to win a Grammy
D) Longest-running song on the Billboard Hot 100

31. Olivia appeared on the cover of Variety magazine at what age?

A) 16
B) 17
C) 18
D) 19

32. What song did Olivia perform when she made her Saturday Night Live debut in 2021?

A) Deja Vu
B) Good 4 U
C) Traitor
D) Drivers License

Extended Trivia!

33. Which phone accessory company did Olivia collaborate with in 2021?

A) Casetify
B) PopSockets
C) OtterBox
D) Spigen

34. What was Olivia's major during her poetry class at USC?

A) Creative Writing
B) Poetry and Lyrics
C) Songwriting
D) Fiction Writing

35. Which song from Guts was based on a poetry class assignment?

A) Lacy
B) Vampire
C) Bad Idea Right?
D) All-American

Extended Trivia!

36. How many tracks did Olivia release as part of Guts: The Secret Tracks?

A) 2
B) 3
C) 4
D) 5

37. Who was Olivia's first co-writer for "Drivers License"?

A) Taylor Swift
B) Jack Antonoff
C) Dan Nigro
D) Conan Gray

38. Olivia often credits which hobby for helping her stay grounded?

A) Baking
B) Knitting
C) Running
D) Journaling

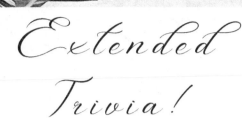

Extended Trivia!

39. Olivia's fashion during the Sour era was inspired by what decade?

A) 1980s
B) 1990s
C) 2000s
D) 2010s

40. Olivia's first headlining tour, Sour Tour, included stops in which countries?

A) United States, United Kingdom, Australia
B) United States, Canada, Europe
C) United States, Mexico, Asia
D) United States, Canada, Japan

41. What was Olivia's first collaboration with a major beauty brand?

A) Glossier
B) Sephora
C) L'Oréal
D) MAC

Extended Trivia!

42. Olivia is often seen wearing which classic shoe brand?

A) Vans
B) Converse
C) Nike
D) Adidas

43. Which of Olivia's songs was recorded and released exclusively for Record Store Day in 2023?

A) Brutal
B) Favorite Crime
C) Guts: The Secret Tracks
D) Jealousy, Jealousy

44. Olivia met with President Joe Biden to promote which cause in 2021?

A) Climate Change
B) Mental Health Awareness
C) Vaccination
D) Animal Rights

Extended Trivia!

43. Which charitable organization did Dolly Parton create to support literacy?

A) Dolly's Book Club
B) Read with Dolly
C) Imagination Library
D) Dolly's Reading Room

45. Olivia cites which singer as her "hero of all heroes"?

A) Lorde
B) Taylor Swift
C) Jack White
D) Billie Eilish

46. What color was the vinyl edition of Olivia's limited Sour release?

A) Blue
B) Green
C) Purple
D) Yellow

Extended Trivia!

47. Which of Olivia's songs includes a phone call as part of its bridge?

A) Get Him Back!
B) Traitor
C) Drivers License
D) Jealousy, Jealousy

48. What is Olivia's go-to relaxing hobby?

A) Knitting
B) Hiking
C) Playing video games
D) Yoga

49. Olivia wrote her first Christmas song when she was how old?

A) 6
B) 5
C) 4
D) 7

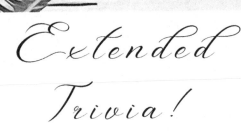
50. Olivia performed at which iconic venue during her Sour tour?

A) Madison Square Garden
B) The Hollywood Bowl
C) The Greek Theatre
D) The O2 Arena

51. Olivia played which character on High School Musical: The Musical: The Series?

A) Gina Porter
B) Gabriella Montez
C) Nini Salazar-Roberts
D) Kourtney Greene

Answers!

1. C) Drivers License
2. B) High School Musical: The Musical: The Series
3. B) 2021
4. C) Deja Vu
5. C) Murrieta
6. A) Red
7. C) Brutal
8. B) Isabel
9. B) Bizaardvark
10. C) No Doubt
11. B) 1 Step Forward, 3 Steps Back
12. C) 12
13. B) Geffen Records
14. C) 3
15. A) Sour Prom
16. B) Avril Lavigne
17. C) Mint Chocolate Chip
18. B) Can't Catch Me Now
19. C) 2010
20. C) 3
21. A) Vampire
22. B) Her parents
23. A) Dorothy McElhinney Middle School
24. D) Good 4 U
25. C) 5 weeks
26. A) Taylor Swift

Answers!

27. B) Musical Theater Program
28. C) 12
29. D) Love is Embarrassing
30. A) Most streams in a single day on Spotify
31. C) 18
32. D) Drivers License
33. A) Casetify
34. B) Poetry and Lyrics
35. A) Lacy
36. C) 4
37. C) Dan Nigro
38. D) Journaling
39. B) 1990s
40. B) United States, Canada, Europe
41. A) Glossier
42. B) Converse
43. C) Guts: The Secret Tracks
44. C) Vaccination
45. C) Jack White
46. C) Purple
47. A) Get Him Back!
48. A) Knitting
49. B) 5
50. C) The Greek Theatre
51. C) Nini Salazar-Roberts

Score Card

Person 1: Score _ _ _ _ _ / 51

Person 2: Score _ _ _ _ _ / 51

Person 3: Score _ _ _ _ _ / 51

Person 4: Score _ _ _ _ _ / 51

Person 5: Score _ _ _ _ _ / 51

Person 6: Score _ _ _ _ _ / 51

Person 7: Score _ _ _ _ _ / 51

Person 8: Score _ _ _ _ _ / 51

Person 9: Score _ _ _ _ _ / 51

Person 10: Score _ _ _ _ _ / 51

20-26: Olivia Fan

You're getting there! As an Olivia Fan, you've shown a lot of love for her music and story. You've learned some cool facts, but there's still more to discover. Keep singing along and diving into her world—you're on your way!

27-33: Rising Olivia Star

Awesome job! You're shining bright, just like Olivia, and you've picked up a lot about her journey so far. You're well on your way to becoming an Olivia pro, but there's still a little more to uncover. Keep that curiosity alive—you're almost there!

34-40: Olivia Enthusiast

Wow, you really know your stuff! You've got a deep understanding of Olivia's life, music, and all the fun details in between. Just a bit more and you'll be at expert level. Keep going—you're so close to mastering all things Olivia!

41-47: Olivia Expert

Incredible! You've mastered the ins and outs of Olivia's journey, from her early days to her biggest hits. Your knowledge is next level, and you're rocking the Olivia world with confidence. Keep this up and you'll be the ultimate Olivia pro!

48-51: Olivia Rodrigo Royalty

Unstoppable! You've reached the peak of Olivia knowledge, and your understanding of her life and career is seriously impressive. You're not just a fan—you're part of Olivia Rodrigo royalty! You know it all, and your passion for her is clear. Keep being awesome!

Dear Reader,

Thank you so much for joining me on this fun ride through "101 Facts About Olivia Rodrigo: The Unofficial Kid and Teen Quiz & Trivia Guide to the Pop Music Sensation." Having you read along has made this project even more special!

Putting this book together was such a blast. Learning all these cool facts about Olivia and seeing how much she inspires others was awesome. Every fact in here is a little piece of what makes Olivia's journey so amazing.

This book was created with love, and it's meant to bring fans who admire Olivia Rodrigo's talent and story together! The moments shared here are all about the passion, joy, and creativity that make Olivia such a

Enjoy the coloring section :)

ıis is me up the top
eft, until next time,
Tessa Temecula

I have added a QR code with the coloring pages that come along with the paperback.

I have also added a downloadable PDF if you would like to print out the book for you and your friends :)

If you are also Interested in Taylor Swift, Dolly Parton or Beyonce and want a digital copy of the book, email us at 101factsaboutstars@gmail.com for more details!

Thank you,

Tessa Temecula

Made in the USA
Las Vegas, NV
18 November 2024

12080104R00066